INVESTIGATING
Conspiracy Theories

Area 51, Lizard People,
AND MORE CONSPIRACY THEORIES ABOUT THE UNEXPLAINED

by Jose Cruz

CAPSTONE PRESS
a capstone imprint

Published by Capstone Press, an imprint of Capstone
1710 Roe Crest Drive, North Mankato, Minnesota 56003
capstonepub.com

Copyright © 2025 by Capstone. All rights reserved. No part of this publication may be reproduced in whole or in part, or stored in a retrieval system, or transmitted in any form or by any means, electronic, mechanical, photocopying, recording, or otherwise, without written permission of the publisher.

Library of Congress Cataloging-in-Publication Data is available on the Library of Congress website.
ISBN: 9781669077329 (hardcover)
ISBN: 9781669077275 (paperback)
ISBN: 9781669077282 (ebook PDF)

Summary: Did an alien spacecraft crash near Roswell, New Mexico, in 1947? Is the U.S. government hiding alien secrets at Area 51? Could lizard people be in positions of power around the world? Conspiracy theories about the paranormal and other unexplained events go hand in hand. Get details about the theories to find out why people believe them and what experts say. Can the conspiracy theories be debunked, or is the truth still out there?

Editorial Credits
Editor: Carrie Sheely; Designer: Jaime Willems; Media Researcher: Svetlana Zhurkin; Production Specialist: Whitney Schaefer

Image Credits
Alamy: Andrew Hasson, 15; Associate Press: File/Idaho Statesman, 9, Susan Walsh, 10; Capstone: Jaime Willems (doodles), cover, back cover, and throughout; Getty Images: AFP/Joshua Roberts, 12, Daemon Barzai, 14, Express/Chris Wood, 4, Mario Tama, 24, Roger Holden, 25, WireImage/Barry King, 28; Newscom: Mirrorpix/Moore Mike, 5, ZUMA Press/Arnie Sachs, 16; Shutterstock: Amy Nichole Harris, 23, Blackday, 19, CloudOnePhoto, cover (bottom right), Fred Mantel, 21, ktsdesign, 26, Mega Pixel (yellow paper), cover, back cover, and throughout, Mwaits, 11, Nikolay Suchkov (color pins), cover, back cover, and throughout, pics five (string and crumpled paper), cover, back cover, and throughout, Pressmaster, 7, Skylines (instant photo), 5, and throughout, Studio Romantic, cover (bottom left), back cover, 1; The Smithsonian Institution: National Air and Space Museum/Transferred from the United States Air Force, 27; SuperStock: ClassicStock, 22, Image Asset Management/World History Archive, 8

Any additional websites and resources referenced in this book are not maintained, authorized, or sponsored by Capstone. All product and company names are trademarks™ or registered® trademarks of their respective holders.

Printed and bound in China. PO 5827

TABLE OF CONTENTS

Chapter 1
What Are Conspiracy Theories? 4

Chapter 2
Aliens Crashed-Landed at Roswell 8

Chapter 3
Reptiles Rule the World 14

Chapter 4
Alien Builders 20

Chapter 5
Area 51 Secrets 24

      Glossary 30
      Read More 31
      Internet Sites 31
      Index 32
      About the Author 32

Words in **BOLD** are in the glossary.

Chapter 1

WHAT ARE CONSPIRACY THEORIES?

In 1966, a banana farmer saw an unidentified flying object (UFO) take off from his land in Queensland, Australia. The object left behind a strange formation in the tall grass. It was one of the first sightings of what came to be known as a crop circle. Soon giant lines, circles, and stars began appearing in fields all over the world, especially in southern England. Many people started to believe that aliens made these designs. Some people thought the designs were messages from aliens. These beliefs soon turned into a conspiracy theory.

An overhead view of crop circles in Wiltshire, England, in 1985

But the truth is that crop circles are not made by aliens. In 1991, Doug Bower and Dave Chorley admitted to creating most of the crop circles in England. Experiments proved that these shapes could easily be made by humans using tools. Yet some people still connect crop circles with aliens today.

Doug Bower shows how he and Dave Chorley created crop circles.

WORKING IN SECRET

The idea that crop circles are made by aliens is an example of a conspiracy theory. A conspiracy theory is a belief that certain events are secretly the work of a hidden group. Governments or other powerful groups are often said to be involved. People think the groups don't have people's best interests in mind. Believers in conspiracy theories often reject official explanations and **evidence** that doesn't support their beliefs. Parts of a conspiracy theory may be true. But the explanations of how or why an event occurred are usually false.

People believe and spread conspiracy theories for different reasons. Spreading these theories can lead to anger, fear, and confusion. Many conspiracy theories are about unexplained happenings. When events are mysterious, they can easily lead to conspiracy theories. Get ready to learn about some of the most popular conspiracy theories about aliens, top-secret places, and more!

Questions to Ask About Conspiracy Theories

- When you find out about a conspiracy theory, do research. Learn as much as you can. It's important not to assume a conspiracy theory is true. Many conspiracy theories can be proven false. For others, parts of them may be true.
- What evidence supports this theory? Ask if there are reliable sources or scientific studies that provide evidence for the claims.
- Who is saying this? What are the sources of information? Consider whether the sources are trustworthy.
- Are there other explanations? Consider different viewpoints. Think critically and weigh different possibilities.
- Has this theory been widely accepted or rejected by experts? Understand the value of expert opinions and scientific evidence. Theories that are widely accepted by experts are generally more reliable than those supported by a few individuals or groups.

Chapter 2

ALIENS CRASHED-LANDED AT ROSWELL

In July 1947, a rancher living near Roswell, New Mexico, discovered strange **debris** on his property. It appeared to be a collection of wood, foil, and rubber. The local Air Force base was notified. Major Jesse Marcel collected the debris and referred to the object as a "flying saucer." According to Marcel's family, Marcel showed them the materials and believed they had come from another world. On July 8, a newspaper included the words "flying saucer" in a headline about the event. Another official quickly stated the object was actually a crashed weather balloon. But some people refused to accept this statement.

The front page of the *Roswell Daily Record* on July 8, 1947

Many UFO Sightings

Pilot Kenneth Arnold reported seeing nine UFOs over Mount Rainier in Washington on June 24, 1947. This started a trend of witnesses reporting similar objects in the sky. That year, more than 850 UFO sightings were reported in national newspapers. It is possible these reports influenced stories about the Roswell crash.

Kenneth Arnold stands outside the plane he piloted when he reported seeing UFOs.

A military official holds a copy of *The Roswell Report*.

As it turned out, the government wasn't telling the truth. But it wasn't because aliens were visiting us. In 1994, the military released information about the Roswell event in *The Roswell Report*. The report said the military had been conducting a top-secret operation called Project MOGUL in 1947. The debris found near Roswell came from a special aircraft. It had sensors and other equipment attached to a balloon. Some of the materials had never been used before, such as fireproof fabrics. The aircraft was designed to help the military find out if the Soviet Union was developing **nuclear** weapons. Admitting what the debris came from would have ruined the military's secret operations.

A CONSPIRACY IS BORN

In 1980, a book called *The Roswell Incident* brought even more attention to the event. It included the first report that the military had hidden alien bodies from the crash.

An engineer named Grady Barnett reported that he discovered dead bodies of small creatures near a crashed saucer. He said he was told not to tell anyone about what he saw.

Some people doubted Barnett's story. His sighting took place about 150 miles (240 kilometers) from Roswell. Barnett was never interviewed directly. All the information came from friends and relatives. Still, Barnett's story was shared on television. This made the conspiracy theory more popular than ever.

Roswell conspiracy theory believers demonstrate in Washington, D.C., in 1995.

Soon books about the bodies said to be found at Roswell were published. The attention they brought kept the conspiracy theory alive. According to a poll, one out of three Americans believes it is possible aliens landed in Roswell. But there isn't solid evidence to support this claim.

A Faked Video

In 1995, a television show aired called *Alien Autopsy: (Fact or Fiction?)*. It showed what it said was video footage of an alien corpse from Roswell being studied. The program was very popular with viewers. But years later, one of the producers admitted that they had staged everything. The alien body had been created by a sculptor using lamb bones from a butcher's shop.

Chapter 3
REPTILES RULE THE WORLD

Could **reptilian** creatures disguised as humans be hidden among us? And could these lizard people have plans for world **domination**? According to a 2013 poll, 12 million Americans believed lizard people were already running the country. How did this strange idea come to be believed by so many?

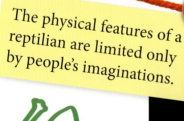

The physical features of a reptilian are limited only by people's imaginations.

David Icke

AN IDEA STARTS

Many fiction books have been written about part-human and part-reptile beings. Versions of the lizard people conspiracy theory have existed for decades. The current version was made popular by former athlete David Icke. In the late 1990s, his book *The Biggest Secret* was published. In it, he said that lizard people are a group of shapeshifters from another **dimension**. He said many world leaders were related to these lizard people. The conspiracy theory grew and spread from these ideas.

Believers claim there are ways to tell if someone is really a lizard person in disguise. These include piercing eyes, body scars, a fascination with science, and the ability to disrupt electrical appliances.

Icke claims that lizard people are controlling the world by disguising themselves as people in power. They shapeshift from lizards to their human forms. People accused of being reptiles have included presidents, prime ministers, and celebrities.

Queen Elizabeth II of the United Kingdom and U.S. President George H. W. Bush were said to be lizard people.

Icke has published many books, created websites, and given presentations to thousands of people about his theory. Over time, many people began to believe these claims. The ability to easily share information on the internet has added to the popularity of the conspiracy theory.

THE CONSPIRACY LIVES ON

Believers have posted dozens of videos online. They study images and videos of politicians and celebrities for signs of shapeshifting. Skeptics point out that video **glitches** might cause someone to appear to shapeshift. There is no proof that anyone is a lizard person in disguise. But this hasn't stopped people from believing the conspiracy theory.

Fact
In 2008, a voter in Minnesota cast their ballot with a write-in choice for "lizard people" as a joke.

The idea of shapeshifting appeared in stories long ago. Today, it's part of popular culture.

Chapter 4

ALIEN BUILDERS

In northern Egypt, three pyramids stand tall near the Nile River. They are known as the Pyramids of Giza. The ancient Egyptians built them more than 4,500 years ago. The pyramids were built as tombs for ancient Egyptian kings, or pharaohs. But was it just human hands that built these impressive structures? Or did the ancient Egyptians have help from aliens?

Some people believe in the ancient astronaut conspiracy theory. This theory suggests that advances of early **civilizations** only happened because humans were helped by aliens. They say ancient civilizations didn't have the technology to build certain structures. Believers of the theory say evidence shows that aliens visited Earth long ago. Ancient artwork supposedly shows UFOs in the sky. Religious texts are said to describe humans meeting aliens.

Some people think aliens could have visited ancient Egypt in large spaceships.

WHAT RESEARCHERS SAY

If ancient civilizations didn't get help from aliens, how did they create such amazing monuments? Researchers have proven that many of the world's most amazing structures could have been made by people.

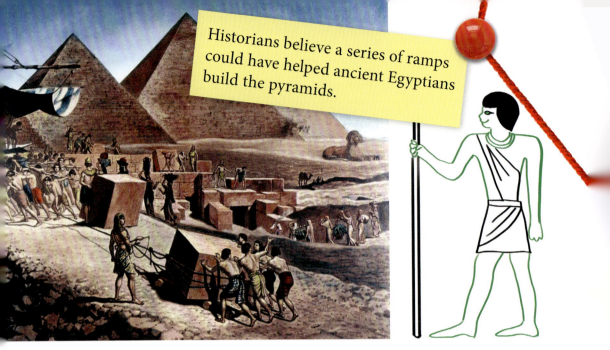

Historians believe a series of ramps could have helped ancient Egyptians build the pyramids.

Conspiracy theory supporters claim only aliens could have built the Pyramids of Giza. They say there wasn't a way for ancient Egyptians to move the massive stones or build such perfect shapes. But experts say it's likely Egyptians used a system of ramps to move the blocks. Research has proven the advanced pyramids **evolved** from simpler burial structures over time.

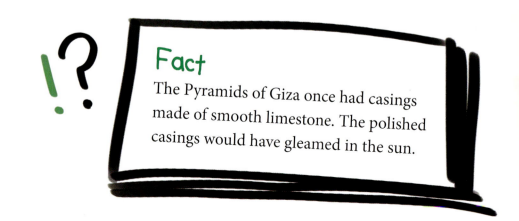

Fact

The Pyramids of Giza once had casings made of smooth limestone. The polished casings would have gleamed in the sun.

The moai of Easter Island are another favorite topic of ancient astronaut theory believers. These carved statues are as tall as 33 feet (10 meters). The heaviest statue weighs more than 80 tons. People living on the island made them between about 1100 and 1650. Scientists think the moai were made in **quarries** before being moved to other places on the island. How could these huge statues be moved? Experts have shown that humans could have moved the statues with nothing but ropes and teamwork.

Many tourists visit Easter Island to see the moai.

Chapter 5

AREA 51 SECRETS

Deep in the Nevada desert lies a top-secret facility maintained by the U.S. Air Force. It is surrounded by gates. Signs warn people not to **trespass**. People call it Area 51. What is the cause of all this secrecy? Is Area 51 a training field for new military aircraft? Or could it be a storage place for alien spacecraft? Conspiracy theorists believe it's both!

People curious about Area 51 often go to the Nevada Test and Training Range entrances.

What's in a Name?

Area 51 is not the true name of the facility. The site is part of the Nevada Test and Training Range. The Central Intelligence Agency officially refers to the site as Homey Airport or Groom Lake. It has also been called Paradise Ranch, Dreamland, and Watertown.

INSIDER STORIES

How did the Area 51 conspiracy theory start? As early as the 1950s, people began reporting UFOs near Area 51. People thought aliens could be flying these UFOs. In 1989, a man named Bob Lazar said he had worked with alien spacecraft in an underground section of the base. Another man claimed he had **telepathically** communicated with an alien creature that was being held at the facility. Other employees reported no knowledge of UFOs at the facility. But the UFO stories soon spread. In the meantime, UFO sightings continued in the area.

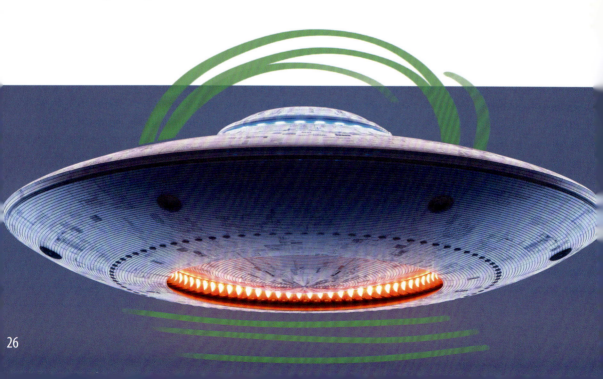

The U-2 flew on its first mission in 1956.

TEST PLANES

Over time, the government started providing some explanations about what was happening at the site. In 1955, the Central Intelligence Agency purchased the airfield that was to become Area 51. The government's plan was to use it to build an advanced spy plane called the U-2. Since then, the site has been used to create other advanced planes.

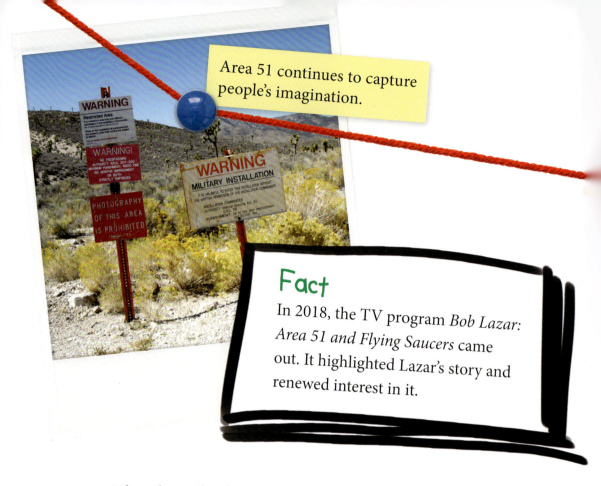

Area 51 continues to capture people's imagination.

Fact
In 2018, the TV program *Bob Lazar: Area 51 and Flying Saucers* came out. It highlighted Lazar's story and renewed interest in it.

The planes built at Area 51 help explain the UFO reports in the area. Oddly shaped, incredibly fast aircraft have likely led witnesses to believe that aliens were traveling nearby.

After Bob Lazar's story became public, some parts of it were not widely believed. It appeared Lazar lied about his education. The government said he never worked at Area 51. Although some people believe alien spaceships could still be at Area 51, there is no real proof.

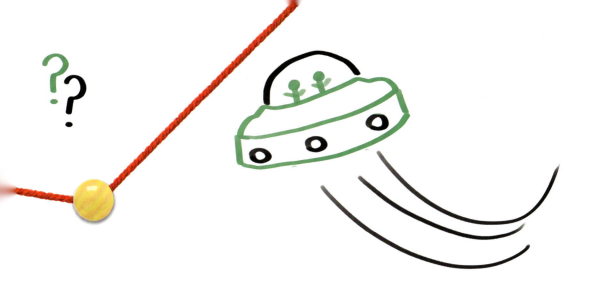

Stories about unexplained events attract interest. It can be fascinating to wonder if a conspiracy theory about them could be true. But it's important to research thoroughly. Often there are more realistic answers to questions conspiracy theories raise. Correcting misinformation is a way to keep it from spreading. The truth is out there, and it's up to you to find it and share it!

Glossary

civilization (si-vuh-luh-ZAY-shuhn)—an organized and advanced society

debris (duh-BREE)—the scattered pieces of something that has been broken or destroyed

dimension (duh-MEN-shuhn)—a universe or reality

domination (dah-muh-NAY-shuhn)—the act of ruling

evidence (EV-uh-duhnss)—information, items, and facts that help prove something to be true or false

evolve (i-VAHLV)—when something develops over a long time with gradual changes

glitch (GLICH)—an unexpected small problem

nuclear (NOO-klee-ur)—having to do with the energy created by splitting atoms; nuclear bombs use this energy to cause an explosion

quarry (KWOR-ee)—a place where stone or other minerals are dug from the ground

reptilian (rep-TI-lee-uhn)—relating to reptiles; reptiles are cold-blooded animals that breathe air and usually have scales

telepathic (te-luh-PA-thik)—able to communicate from one mind to another without speech or signs

trespass (TRESS-pass)—to enter someone's private property without permission

Read More

Doeden, Matt. *What Are Hoaxes and Lies?* Minneapolis: Lerner, 2020.

Hubbard, Ben. *What Do We Know About the Roswell Incident?* New York: Penguin Workshop, 2023.

Kim, Carol. *Area 51 Alien and UFO Mysteries.* North Mankato, MN: Capstone, 2022.

Internet Sites

BBC: What Is Area 51 and What Goes on There?
bbc.com/news/world-us-canada-49568127

Kiddle: Roswell Incident Facts for Kids
kids.kiddle.co/Roswell_incident

Wonderopolis: What Are Crop Circles?
wonderopolis.org/wonder/what-are-crop-circles

Index

aliens, 4, 5, 6, 10, 11, 13, 20, 21, 22, 24, 26, 28
Area 51, 24, 25, 26, 27, 28
Arnold, Kenneth, 9

Barnett, Grady, 11, 12

Central Intelligence Agency, 25, 27
crop circles, 4, 5, 6

Easter Island, 23

Icke, David, 15, 16, 17

Lazar, Bob, 26, 28
lizard people, 14, 15, 16, 18

Marcel, Jesse, 8
moai, 23

Nevada Test and Training Range, 24, 25

Project MOGUL, 10
Pyramids of Giza, 20, 22

shapeshifting, 15, 16, 18, 19

U-2 planes, 27
UFOs, 4, 9, 20, 26, 28

About the Author

Jose Cruz is an elementary school media specialist based in Southwest Florida. His journalism and short fiction have appeared in print and online, including best-of collections. His favorite topics deal with the dark, the strange, and the mysterious.